Piano
Initial

Pieces & Exercises
for Trinity College London exams

2015-2017

Published by
Trinity College London Press
www.trinitycollege.com

Registered in England
Company no. 09726123

Printed in England by Caligraving Ltd.

Gavotte

(optional duet part)

Arr. Carol Barratt

James Hook
(1746-1827)

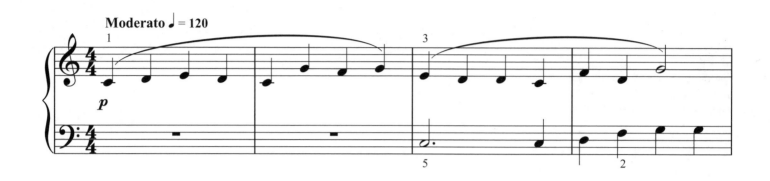

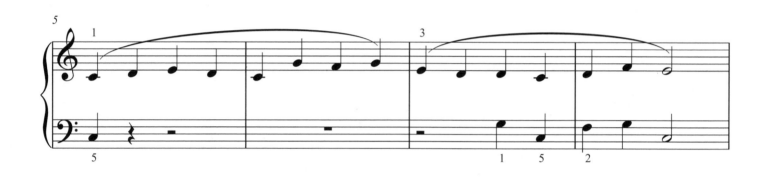

Gavotte

(candidate solo part)

Arr. Carol Barratt

James Hook
(1746-1827)

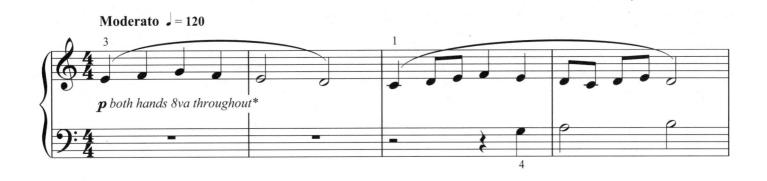

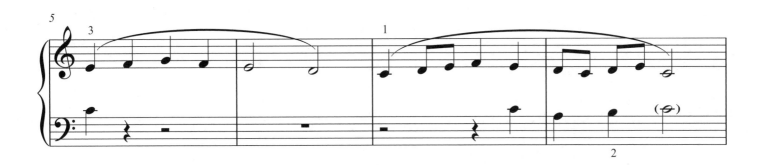

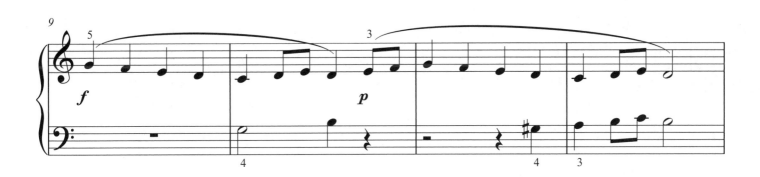

* duet performance only

Summer Swing

Ed. Peter Wild

August Eberhard Müller
(1767–1817)

March Time

Wilhelm Moritz Vogel
(1846-1922)

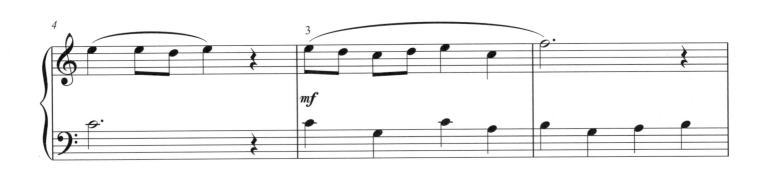

On a Wintry Day

Dulcie Holland
(1913-2000)

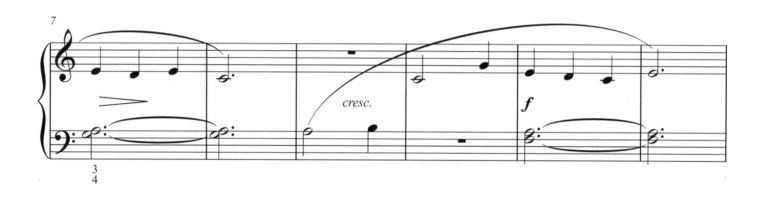

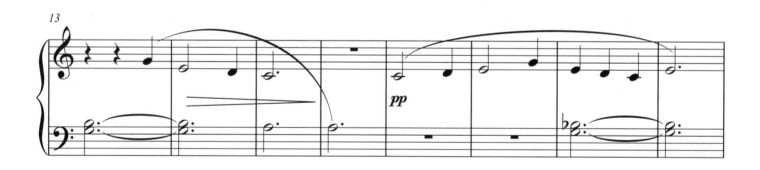

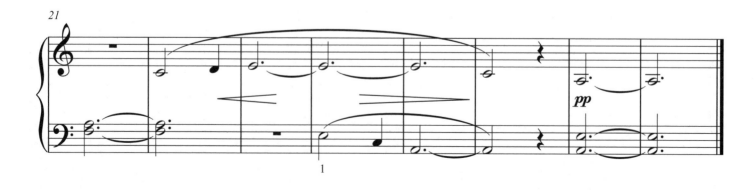

Easy Living

Kay Charlton
(born 1963)

Spring Day

(optional duet part)

Christopher Norton
(born 1945)

Spring Day

(candidate solo part)

Christopher Norton
(born 1945)

The Stroke of Midnight

Sarah Walker
(born 1965)

Smooth and Crunchy

Elissa Milne
(born 1967)

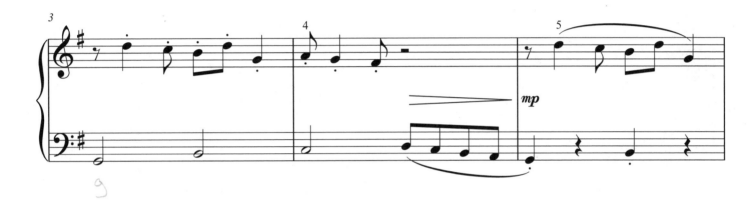

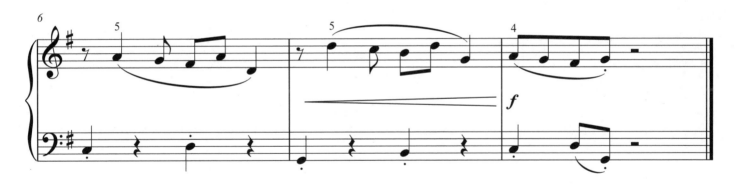

Composer's original metronome mark is ♩ = 138

Ready To Go!

Ben Crosland
(born 1968)

Composer's original metronome mark is ♩ = 104

Exercises

1a. Snow Flakes – tone, balance and voicing

1b. Change of mind – tone, balance and voicing

2a. Sad Moment – co-ordination

13

2b. Last One In! – co-ordination

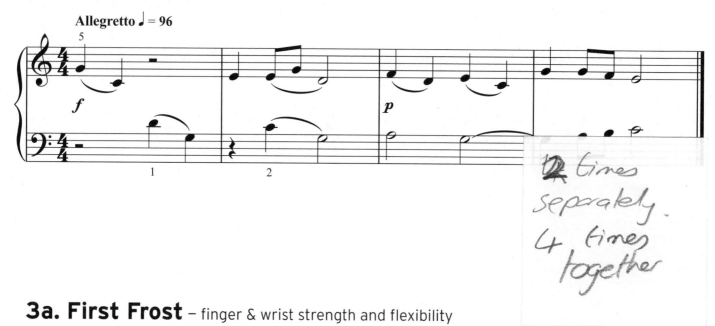

(handwritten note) 2 times separately. 4 times together

3a. First Frost – finger & wrist strength and flexibility

3b. Relay Race – finger & wrist strength and flexibility